This Book Belongs To:

Made in the USA
Monee, IL
07 July 2026

56550177R00057